"Even in the face of today's rapid inflation, it is possible to serve adequate, nourishing meals on a small budget — and it can be done without sacrificing attractiveness, variety or hospitality. I've written LOVE IS . . . JELLY ON THE BREAD to show you how."

Charlotte U. Syme

# Love Is...
# Jelly on the
# Bread

Charlotte U. Syme

 ACCENT BOOKS
Denver, Colorado

MEMBER OF
EVANGELICAL CHRISTIAN
PUBLISHERS ASSOCIATION

ACCENT BOOKS
A division of Accent-B/P Publications, Inc.
12100 W. Sixth Avenue
P.O. Box 15337
Denver, Colorado 80215

Library of Congress Catalog Card Number: 78-59934

ISBN 0-89636-010-5

# Contents

*TO GEORGE*
*because he always says,*
*"That was delicious!"*
*in a way that makes me*
*believe him*

# Come In
# and Welcome

**A** child was asked to define lovingkindness. "Well," he said thoughtfully, "when I come in from school and ask for a snack, if my mom gives me bread and butter, that's kindness. If she spreads jelly on it, that's lovingkindness."

A popular cartoon would express it: "Love is . . . putting jelly on the bread." Spreading jelly is an *action* and, to one child at least, an action that says, "I love you."

Love is always described in the Bible as an act—never as an emotion. Love is most often illustrated with action verbs: "God so loved . . . that he gave . . ." (John 3:16); "God commendeth his love . . . in that . . . Christ died . . ." (Romans 5:8); "If ye love me, keep my commandments" (John 14:15); "Charity [love] suffereth . . . rejoiceth . . . beareth . . . believeth . . . hopeth . . . endureth" (I Corinthians 13:4-7). These verses express even the negative as action—from "envieth not" to "never faileth."

The kitchen is a wonderful place for showing love through actions. Even stringent economic circumstances can illustrate it. A man who grew up in the depression years liked to tell of the Christmas his family could only afford hot dogs. With a few toothpicks and a loving imagination, the mother brought them to the table cleverly disguised as a platter of animals. The children remembered that dinner long after many stuffed turkeys had been eaten and forgotten. Love provides the jelly, creates centerpieces, remembers likes and dislikes, plans for variety, and makes each meal a thank offering to the One who has given us those we love.

This is not principally a book of recipes although there are some contained herein. Rather, it is a sharing of suggestions gleaned over more than thirty years of preparing meals on a careful budget while striving to make them both nutritious and attractive.

In a time when economy is becoming a major factor in many homes, and when young Christians are being encouraged to develop a simpler lifestyle, especially as to their eating habits, it may be that my experiences will spark your own ingenuity. And, hopefully, the accompanying bits of meditation will encourage you to remember that your job is one where you are privileged to work in partnership with the Creator of every good and perfect gift designed for our daily needs.

So, come in and welcome! There is confusion and crowding here, and my equipment is sinking into old age. But it has kept my husband and three children (now grown) in good health, with good appetites. Besides—I love having guests!

# 1
# Soup for Practically Nothing

My friend had six children and it took most of his paycheck and all of his wife's ingenuity to keep the plates filled. There came a day when, for a reason I forget, he took the whole family out for the rare and wonderful treat of a restaurant dinner.

The adults and older children ordered soup for the first course, an item not included with the youngsters' menus. It was delivered promptly. As they waited for their dinner plates, the little ones watched the soup go down and finally one piped up, "You will wait for us after you've finished, won't you?"

"You see," their mother explained when describing the incident, "when they have soup at home, that's the whole meal."

Making soup the "whole meal" is still an unequaled budget-stretcher, provided it is hearty enough to leave your diners with a sense of contentment. During the fall chills and winter freezes, you can feature the steaming bowls at least once a week.

Three soups are most likely to be served at my table. One begins with browned beef stock. I make it when I find a beef knuckle or the trimmed ends of short ribs being sold for a pittance, or when I have a piece of pot roast or chuck steak from which I have trimmed the ragged and bony ends.

These odds and ends are well browned along with a sliced onion, then simmered until the meat falls away from the bone. A bay leaf, a stalk of celery and a carrot (both sliced), a little parsley, and salt and pepper to taste should simmer along with the meat and onion. I like to add a beef bouillon cube or, when I have it, an envelope of beefy onion soup powder.

The soup chapter of your cookbook will have several recipes which start with this beef stock. My favorite ingredients to add to the beef stock are barley, a jar of tomatoes, any leftover vegetables and vegetable liquid in the refrigerator and, of course, seasoning to taste.

The bone and gristly scraps from a picnic shoulder ham make my husband's favorite soup dish. You will want to put in the pot with the scraps, a bay leaf, some thyme or celery leaves, and four or five whole cloves, unless you originally cooked the meat with cloves, in which case there are probably some among the leftover scraps. After simmering, strain the stock and save any good bits of ham.

Use this stock to make a smooth, green split pea soup. A blender will make the job easy for you. I do not have one but have no trouble stirring the soup smooth once the peas have simmered to the mushy stage. Yellow peas or lentils also make delicious variations, but will not save as many pennies as the green peas will.

Serve this soup sprinkled with grated cheese or with croutons made of cubed bread fried in margarine or oil and sprinkled with garlic salt or grated cheese. If you have a leftover hot dog in the refrigerator, cut it into rings and float them on the green sea. The soup can also be served in bouillon cups as the first course of a company meal. It looks very festive topped with a dollop of sour cream.

My third and most frequent soup pot is a vegetable soup with a chicken or turkey stock base. There is always something in my freezer for making it. It may be a collection of packaged giblets, necks, wing tips and other leftover odds and ends from whole birds. (We will talk about planning for these odds and ends in "The Versatile Chicken.") Where I live, packaged chicken or turkey backs and necks sell for between ten and twenty cents a pound. These make excellent stock bases.

To make the stock, I add onion, the *stem* ends of two or three carrots, bits of greens that are a little too tired-looking for salad, celery leaves, and thyme or poultry seasoning. After the stock has been simmered and strained, I add rice or noodles, a jar of tomatoes and a package or can of corn or mixed vegetables. I never pass up a sale on these items. When possible, I slice a few okra into it. We grow half a dozen okra plants in our small garden every summer just for this purpose, but the supply is not sufficient to last long into the winter.

My favorite crowning touch is a few grains of saffron which adds an unbelievably rich look to the finished product. Yes, I know saffron is the most expensive spice on the market, but perhaps my one claim to fame is that I possess what may be a lifetime supply. My daughter brought it home and taught me to use it after a teaching stint in Spain, where it sells for pennies and is a staple in every kitchen. A small pinch of turmeric will give a similar effect.

With this last soup you have a bonus. You may, especially if it is turkey, get two to three cups of meat when you clean off the bones. After you put a half cup or so into the soup, you will have enough left to make a casserole, a la king or chop suey. Presto—another meal! Or you may prefer chicken or turkey salad sandwiches. My husband likes the livers mashed with a little mayonnaise, salt and pepper, minced onion, celery, green pepper, or whatever crunchy item I have, and a bit of pickle relish for a sandwich spread.

At our house, the gizzards and hearts, along with the odds and ends of skin, serve the dog. But there are giblet recipes in any standard cookbook if you want to go the last mile in economy. I have done so and they can be quite tasty if they are cooked very tender and are not served too often.

When soup is the main dish, I serve it with a substantial salad and with either a good homemade bread—always appreciated—or garlic bread made from a French or Italian loaf picked up on the day-old rack. A tossed green salad with slivers of cheese, or a fruit or gelatin salad served with cottage cheese boost the protein value of the meal. For dessert, this is the type of dinner where I indulge my craving for richer ones, topping it off with a favorite cake or pie.

My children are not often at home now—two are married and one is in college—but when any of them are around, they still look for snacks. One evening while investigating my refrigerator, one of them spied a jar of leftover chicken-vegetable soup and asked, "Do you have plans for that or can I heat it up?" If I had had plans, I would have changed them forthwith. It is a memory I cherish.

# 2
# The Heavenly Dinner Table

The God-given privilege of nourishing human bodies which are temples of the Holy Spirit can be accomplished for His glory. If at times it seems monotonous or unappreciated, we may remind ourselves that our Heavenly Father has set the example by making available to His family the perfect and complete diet to feed lives destined for eternity. "Man doth not live by bread only," He said, "but by every word that proceedeth out of the mouth of the Lord doth man live" (Deuteronomy 8:3b).

What a well-rounded menu He provides! It includes bread, Jesus reminded us (Luke 4:4)—the staff of life, the basic grain food all men need. For His new babes and growing children, it includes rich and abundant milk—easily taken in and digested (I Peter 2:2).

For the active youth and hard-working adult, He provides solid protein-rich meat. It may need to be well-chewed before it can be properly digested, but its assimilation builds the strong muscle of mature Christian character (Hebrews 5:12-14). Then, as special evidence of His love, He has added dessert for the spiritual sweet tooth, making His Word "sweeter also than honey and the honeycomb" (Psalm 19:10b). This food, along with bodily sustenance, ought to be the constant diet of even young children (Deuteronomy 6:7).

*To meditate on: Are those I feed receiving spiritual meals as nourishing and attractive as their physical ones? Dear Lord, keep me aware that You have entrusted me with lives to be fed for eternity as well as for time.*

*LOVE IS Jelly on the Bread*

# 3
# Treat and Save
# with Tuna

Parenthood has its unexpected small surprises. I like to remember the day my daughter phoned from her college dormitory to tell me she would be home for the weekend, then added, "I'm bringing two girl friends to help celebrate my birthday. Is that okay?"

I assured her it was and asked what she wanted to eat. It was traditional for each of the children to select the dinner menu on his or her birthday. Since I had become inured to such budget-busting requests as thick steak, large shrimp, or pizza from the pizza parlor "with everything," I held my breath. I nearly dropped the phone when she replied, "How about one of your nice tuna fish casseroles?"

Since that occasion I have never hesitated to serve tuna fish, even to company. From long before that it had been one of my favorite budget-shrinkers. The children have eaten it once or twice a week throughout their lives. The fact that it remains a favorite food with all of them says much for the amount of variety possible in its preparation. Often only minor changes are required to achieve it.

For my daughter's birthday, I served it as a

casserole consisting of noodles, tomato sauce flavored with chopped onion, peppers and celery seed, and topped it with a design of sliced American cheese.

Macaroni, which is more economical, may be substituted for the noodles. Instead of tomato sauce, a medium white sauce may be used—or to save time instead of money, canned cream of mushroom or cream of celery soup. Pimento, sliced black or green olives, or parsley may be added to the white sauce. A quarter cup of mayonnaise added to white sauce gives it a gourmet taste, as do chopped almonds or cashews. Do-it-yourself flavored bread cubes or crumbs make a tasty, crunchy topping.

On a hot, summer day, a bowl of tuna-macaroni salad makes a filling and nourishing main dish. It invariably brings expressions of pleasure in our house. In addition to mayonnaise, it may be tossed with celery seed, sliced black and/or green olives, and any available crisp, chopped vegetable, such as green peppers, celery or radishes. Since we like a hint of onion, I sometimes use scallion tops or chives. If they are not available, a sprinkle of onion salt does very nicely.

Again, nuts are a nice addition for a special occasion. For eye appeal, ring with lettuce and sprinkle with paprika or decorate with one or two of the following: tomatoes, cucumbers, peppers, radishes, parsley, olives or hard-boiled eggs.

Tuna salad, either with or without macaroni, may also be served in hollowed-out peppers or tomatoes. My rule of thumb is two cups each of macaroni and sauce for every small can of tuna. This will make four servings, or even six if your vegetables, salad, and dessert are substantial. However, when I had three teenagers at my table, I used a nine and a quarter size can of tuna and increased the other ingredients to three cups.

For a change from macaroni products, you might like to try an upside-down tuna pie. This requires a can of tuna, a quarter cup or more of peas (a good use for leftovers) and a little chopped celery. Moisten ingredients with white or tomato sauce, and top with a recipe of corn muffins or biscuits. Serve it in wedges and pass extra sauce.

Canned salmon or mackerel can be substituted for tuna in any of these dishes. Canned mackerel is the most economical, but your family's taste preferences should be your guide. Wasted food saves nothing.

So, stretch your imagination, shrink your budget and enjoy your tuna. Even if your daughter does not request it on her birthday, your son might ask for a recipe to take to his bachelor apartment. Mine did, and later gave it to his wife.

# 4
# Why Salt?

**P**erhaps, since I have somewhat of a sweet tooth, it is a purely personal idiosyncrasy, but I used to wonder sometimes why our Lord called us Christians the salt of the earth rather than the sugar of the earth. After all, should not right Christian living pour sweetness into our human relationships? Still, I reasoned, too much sweet can be cloying and unhealthful.

I stopped wondering after I had occasion to do a little reading on the uses of salt while writing a Sunday School lesson on Matthew 5. For the first time I realized what a basic commodity it is in much of our manufacturing and industry. Its value is such that there have been times throughout history when it was accepted as a medium of exchange.

There are three properties of salt, I learned, that have been known since ancient times and are by themselves sufficient to explain why the people of God are the salt of the earth.

*Salt heals.* It is an important ingredient in many medicinal preparations. It is particularly useful for encouraging the healing of wounds and the destruction of germs, as in gargles.

*Salt preserves.* It is necessary to the process of smoking meat and was essential to the preservation of food long before the days of refrigeration. Even today, the salting of fish and curing of meat provides a major market outlet for salt.

*Salt flavors.* How flat our food is without it! How quickly we notice when the cook has forgotten it. Even when other seasonings are used we cannot omit salt, and if no others are available it is, in itself, sufficient to secure a palatable dish. No wonder Jesus called His people the salt of the earth!

*To meditate on: Am I functioning as good salt in my world, and especially in my family relationships? Does my Christian presence work to cure what is amiss, preserve what is good, and flavor all my relationships? Dear Lord, help me to function as good salt You can pour out for the healing of wounds, preserving of love, and right seasoning of every relationship in my family and community.*

# 5
# The Versatile
# Chicken

This is not intended to be a book about birthdays, but such special occasions do seem to figure largely in the raising and feeding of families and, hence, stick in the memory. During one of his college years, my older son suggested he would like to bring two carloads of friends up for dinner on his birthday. I was agreeable but cautioned him that I would not be able to provide steaks (his usual request) for that many. "That's all right," he assured me. "I'll settle for barbecued chicken."

Chicken is probably one of the best friends an economy-minded homemaker can have. It is always a good buy and frequently a sale item. Not even the much-glorified hamburger can outdo it for stretch-ability and versatility. No matter how often you serve it, you need not repeat the same recipes except by choice.

Every standard cookbook has several pages of chicken recipes. Not a month goes by without the food section of our newspaper giving one or two more. The outside labels of food staples often include new ideas for cooking chicken. There are whole cookbooks devoted to it. Not long ago when the women of my church collected their favorite recipes into a book, I counted no less than thirteen chicken dishes, none of which were exactly like any in my food file.

Chicken recipes run the gamut from those which will fit the tightest budget to some elegant enough to impress your in-laws or your husband's boss. Perhaps it would be appropriate at this point to confess that I generally avoid serving chicken to a preacher—especially a visiting one who is holding meetings and "eating around." It may be that my reason is archaic, but when I was growing up in the South I often heard such preachers, including my father, complain because they were served chicken night after night without a break.

If you are really pinching, you can stretch one fryer into a dinner for ten or twelve by taking all the meat off the frame and using it in a casserole, meat pie or chop suey dish. As an added bonus, the broth you cooked it in can be used as the basis for a tasty first course, or as a main dish soup for the next day's dinner.

Even without being that stringent, you can get valuable extra mileage from your bird without depriving your family of a good plate of fried chicken. Unless there is a very special buy on cut-up chicken, I buy mine whole, thus saving several cents a pound. Cutting a chicken up at home is only a few minutes' work once you have mastered the simple technique. Served fried, the most one chicken will feed is five, especially if they are in the hearty appetite ages. If the number at dinner exceeds that, I use two or more birds, frying the most popular pieces from both.

Learning to separate a chicken into its parts is

very simple. After two or three times you can do it almost without thinking. Begin by removing the wings at the point where they join the body. The joint is severed very easily with a butcher knife. Then take off the legs where they join the thighs, and then take the thighs from the body. All this is a simple matter of separation at joints. Divide the body at the sides, where the ribs separate, into front and back halves, and then the back into its upper and lower parts by a smart blow of the butcher knife to break the backbone just below the ribs.

The front takes a little more explaining, but is easier to do than to describe. It can be simply split in half, but I like to make three pieces of it, so I first remove the meaty wishbone section by placing it skin side up and running a thin paring knife under the wishbone and lifting it off whole with its meat. The remaining piece then requires only to be split lengthwise by splitting the long thin breast cartilage with the point of a sharp paring knife and finishing the rest with a good whack of the butcher knife. (If you have a meat cleaver it is even simpler.)

The entire process is the work of maybe five minutes. My mother showed it to me just once and I have never found it a problem.

My whole chickens usually divide into eleven pieces—the wishbone, and two each of breast, wing, thigh, leg and back. After setting aside the pieces I intend to fry, I consign the remaining pieces to the freezer, dividing them into one of three separate plastic bags always waiting there. The giblets, neck and wing tips go into one bag. Eventually they will become soup stock. The wings go into a separate bag. When I have accumulated enough for a meal (about four wings per serving), I cook them in either a barbecue or oriental sauce and serve with rice.

The backs and any other unused pieces go into the third bag. These, too, are used for soup stock, but after they are simmered, and some meat has been reserved for the finished soup, there is usually still enough to serve another dinner by making a casserole, salad, chicken pie, a la king, chop suey, or, if there are lunches to pack, a nice bowl of sandwich filling. Chicken salad sandwiches are tastier and far less expensive than packaged luncheon meats.

After that, my husband gets the liver, of which he is especially fond. Since our house contains a dog who must be included in the family food budget, the other items are dedicated to him. (Wulfie has also thrived for a dozen years on chicken bones, but since the very suggestion fills dog experts with horror, I do not put it into print as a recommendation, but only as the experience of one lone canine.)

We belong to a book discussion group which meets half a dozen times a year and rotates among the homes of the members, with the hostess providing the main dish for a buffet supper intermission. I once overheard the group chairman telling a guest that the only qualifications for membership were to read the books selected and to know a different way to cook hamburger. I felt that he might have added "or chicken" since it turns up nearly as often and in as many different ways.

This group varies from twelve to twenty at any given meeting. Among the dishes I have served are two chicken recipes I learned from my daughter after her sojourn in Madrid. For Spanish authenticity, the chicken pieces should be cut smaller than the eleven sections I mentioned above. Breasts can be cut cross-wise in halves or thirds depending on their size, and thighs cut in half. Legs can be separated just below the thick bulbous portion and the "sticks" added to your soup bag.

Fry the chicken pieces with an onion and sliced garlic bud. Remove the garlic when browned. To be authentically Spanish, use olive oil; to economize, use a brand that is ten percent olive oil. Stir in a pinch or two of saffron. You can increase it as much as your taste and pocketbook dictate, or save by substituting turmeric or even yellow food coloring (which will imitate the color but not the flavor).

To make *Arroz con Pollo,* add about one quarter cup of rice and one half cup of water per person to the fried chicken. Stir well and cook covered over low heat until the rice is tender and the chicken cooked through.

For the second Spanish chicken dish, *Pollo al Chilindron,* add canned or cubed fresh tomatoes to the browned chicken and onions and an equal amount of green peppers cut into fairly large chunks. The sauce will be thicker if this is simmered uncovered. Serve rice separately. This is a nice dish to have when peppers are inexpensive or, if you have a garden, when your plants are producing abundantly.

For a special occasion, try this oriental dish that always wins compliments. It is not original but gradually has been adapted from several variations. Brown chicken pieces, then simmer covered until tender in a mixture of one cup sweet mixed pickles, one quarter cup pickle liquid, one quarter cup water, two tablespoons soy sauce, a can of pineapple chunks with juice and one teaspoon of salt.

During the last few minutes, add another quarter cup of pickle liquid and a tomato cut in wedges. If tomatoes are out of season, omit them and substitute a bit of pimento or frozen bell pepper for color. If sauce seems thin, thicken with a little cornstarch.

Sometimes I substitute canned mandarin oranges or fresh orange sections and juice for the pineapple, and halved black olives for the pickles. Serve with rice.

One of my boys took *Arroz con Pollo* to school when his Spanish class was assigned to bring in a Spanish menu item. It was not quite authentic. We used only wings and backs, cutting the chicken into bite size bits so there would be a spoonful for everyone to taste without bankrupting us. Thus, we found one more way of turning a little chicken into a substantial and pleasing dinner. Adapting a foreign dish is a good old American custom!

*LOVE IS Jelly on the Bread*

# 6
# Made in His Image

Paul Bocuse, a successful chef, has been quoted as saying, "Use recipes as inspirations: never give up on one if you are lacking an ingredient or two." It is the ability to substitute, to rearrange, to produce new combinations that is the real secret of successful cooking. It is as much an expression of creativity as is painting a picture, writing a poem, or decorating a room.

Every one of us is creative, but some develop their creativity more than others. In Genesis 1, the only thing that God has revealed to us about Himself at that point is that He is the Creator. Then, His expressions of creativity are described. The crowning one is that He created us in His own image (Genesis 1:27). Whatever else that may say about us, it certainly means that we have been endowed with creativity. And what we are given, we are responsible to develop and share.

This does not mean we are necessarily to achieve public acclaim for our contributions to art or to engineering or to some other recognized creative pursuit. If the One to whom we are committed has placed us in our home, at the center of a family, our responsibility is to bring beauty into the lives of our loved ones and to develop their sense of appreciation, imagination and creativity by the sensitivity with which we dress them, decorate for them, and—yes, cook for them.

We do not get very far beyond Genesis 1 before we begin to learn that God is love. It is because we were created in His image that we, too, are capable of loving. This attribute is also necessary to real success in preparing food for a family. Another successful cook, Alain Chapel, recognized this truth by saying, "You have to love either what you are going to eat or the person you are cooking for . . . Cuisine is an act of love."

*To meditate on: Am I learning to use God's gifts of creativity and love to glorify the place He has given me in this home? Dear Lord, may I be alert to finding ways of creating beauty and demonstrating love by my daily tasks, and may I, by my example, develop in my children the creative gift and ability to love that which you have bestowed on them.*

# 7
# The Bountiful
# Casserole

In a letter to my college student son I mentioned that, in line with today's emphasis on simpler living, I was working on a book that I hoped would inspire some creative economy in the kitchen. Writing back, he replied, "I think you should devote at least a chapter to your casseroles."

According to Webster, a casserole is a mold of boiled rice, potatoes or pasta (macaroni or noodle products) baked with meat or vegetables. Admittedly, that does not have an inspired ring and it could produce a dish that is extremely blah. But the possibilities for variation are almost endless, and a little creative attention to combinations of color and flavor can produce a dish that wins "more" requests from your family and appreciative compliments from your guests.

Since there are casserole suggestions scattered throughout this book in chapters concerning such specific subjects as tuna, chicken and meat, this section will deal only with some basic principles which can be adapted to any food. They should be especially helpful for stretching small quantities or recycling leftovers.

Essential to any casserole is a sauce for binding all the ingredients together. If your lifestyle places convenience above economy, there are several varieties of canned soup which make good sauces. Just add half a can of milk to the contents. Or you can learn to make two basic sauces, both of which are adaptable to a variety of casseroles.

The first is a good medium white sauce. It can be used as is, or transformed by the addition of cheese to taste, mushrooms or celery. The white sauce, plain or fancy, is your basis for creamed vegetables, meats, or meat-vegetable combinations, scalloped dishes, and macaroni and cheese. When using this sauce with macaroni products, you will want to add a little color for eye appeal. A few leftover peas, some pimento, or sliced or halved black olives will do very nicely—especially with poultry or seafood casseroles. I keep a large jar of chopped salad olives on hand for this purpose and because some of my family are very fond of cream cheese and olive sandwiches.

Olives are an economic buy. By carefully selecting the reddest-looking jar on the grocer's shelf, I can always extract sufficient pimento for whatever garnish or bit of color I want to add to casseroles or salads.

Tomato sauce is also good in most casseroles. You can often buy good sauces at relatively low cost if you watch for sales or coupon offers. Tomato soup straight from the can serves well as a sauce.

Since I can a quantity of tomatoes, I make my tomato casserole sauce. I brown an onion and a green pepper very lightly in a little fat, then add a jar of tomatoes with a small can of tomato paste or a quarter to third cup of ketchup, simmer until it is not watery, and salt and pepper to taste. If you are in a hurry, you can omit the paste and thicken it quickly with cornstarch.

This basic sauce may be varied with the addition of scallion tops, chopped celery or celery salt, or other preferred spices or herbs. Sometimes I add oregano and grated Italian cheese.

Another essential to an attractive casserole is the topping. Cheese may be either grated over the surface or sliced into attractive patterns. Let it brown and bubble a bit in the oven, but not too much. My other favorite is bread crumbs or cubes browned in margarine or meat fat, and flavored with garlic salt or grated cheese.

If your casserole consists of meat and/or vegetables without rice, pasta or potatoes, then biscuit or corn bread dough makes a nice topping. In this event, you simply change the name from casserole to Upside Down Pie! Biscuits can be given extra zest with parsley flakes, onion or garlic salt, celery seed, or cheese. You can also add interesting flavor by using rendered chicken fat for shortening. (Please note: This book makes no pretense of dealing with either diets or the fear of cholesterol, but only with one family's way of getting maximum mileage from all that the Lord provides.)

You want to be very sure your biscuit topping is well cooked before serving. A gummy underside can deflate the most expectant appetite. A slightly lower temperature and longer cooking time than you use for plain biscuits will insure their being well cooked without becoming overly browned. This is especially important if you spread the dough solidly over the top. But even if you top the casserole with individual biscuits, you will want to peek at the undersides before serving.

Leftover mashed potatoes also make a good topping. Rewhip them with a little additional milk and butter. You may add an egg also, a particularly good idea if the meat content of your dish is minimal. If desired, stir in bits of onion, onion salt, or cheese. Spread over casserole mixture and sprinkle generously with paprika. Then bake. If you don't use paprika, put it briefly under the broiler just before serving for good color.

Any of these casseroles is a one-dish meal. All you need to serve with it is a tossed green salad and a dessert. These dishes also have the added advantage of time flexibility. If you work or have a heavily scheduled day coming up, you can put one together early in the morning, or even the night before, and move it from the refrigerator to the oven half an hour before dinner time.

*LOVE IS Jelly on the Bread*

# 8
# Food for
# the Strong

Haven't you frequently heard Christians, even some who have been Christians for twenty, thirty or forty years, say, "That preacher (or teacher) is over my head—I like to hear the plain and simple gospel"? No doubt Christians such as these were in Paul's mind when he complained that he was still feeding them milk when they ought to be eating meat (Hebrews 5:12-14).

How careful we are about helping our children become accustomed to eating meat! We lead them from milk to strained meat, then to hamburger, and finally to steak. Most healthy children are clamoring for the steak by the time they have their second teeth. Occasionally, however, there is one who resists the new and coarser texture and wants to stay with his accustomed diet. The wise mother does not give in, but gradually and persistently leads him to acceptance of the new level of difficulty.

There are portions of God's Word which might give a newborn child of God an attack of spiritual indigestion. For the spiritual infant to tackle Daniel's seventy weeks or the paradox of God's sovereignty and man's free will can and has caused serious difficulties, whereas any child of God can assimilate John 3:16 or Philippians 4:8.

The children in a Christian home should not be nourished on a twelve-year diet of spiritual baby food and then be expected to cope like strong men with the spiritual battles of the teens. By the time they reach this age, they should be equipped with the powerful spiritual muscles developed by feeding on the meat of the Word.

It, of course, must be given in careful stages. For example, one does not tell a Sunday School beginner that God is omnipresent and omniscient. We teach him that God is with him all the time and knows everything he does and thinks. We try to make it clear that it is not because the Lord is spying to get something against us, but because He loves us so much He can't take His eyes off us. By the time the beginner reaches junior age, he will delight in being able to use and explain the bigger words. And, more important, their significance will be assimilated and become a part of him even through periods of seeming indifference or rebellion.

*To meditate on: Have I been lazy about chewing, or is my Scripture diet such as to make me a strong parent or teacher? Dear Lord, give me the wisdom to provide for myself and my family a diet sturdy enough to turn flabby spiritual muscles into strong, effective ones.*

# 9
# Minimum Meat— Maximum Meal

"Oh, boy! Macaroni and cheese!" How often over the years I have heard this remark as we gathered for dinner. Actually, I do not have a family that takes kindly to meatless meals. Macaroni and cheese was one exception and I served it frequently—sometimes as often as once a week.

Almost everyone is aware that there is no better way to effect a noticeable economy in the food budget than by cutting down on meat. It has been estimated that up to fifty percent of the typical householder's food bill is spent at the meat counter. A secret of good planning, therefore, is to learn ways of cutting down in this department without making your family feel deprived or robbing them of essential protein.

Over the years I have collected a number of meat-stretching meals that are tasty and nourishing. Hamburger is probably the most frequently used budget-balancer. There are several good books and pamphlets on the market devoted entirely to the subject. After studying a number of these recipes, you may discover that you can do an even better job of creating than they do without sacrificing flavor.

The first thing to do with hamburger is to buy it on sale! In my area a number of stores make it their featured "come on" every few weeks—and not all of them the same week! The price drops ten and sometimes twenty cents a pound. Depending on what I can invest, I buy a package from three pounds up, divide it into meal-size portions, and freeze it.

One half pound of hamburger will make a large pot of chili or spaghetti sauce, or cabbage rolls for four. To make the last, combine the meat with a cup of rice, salt, pepper, minced onion and grated cheese to taste. Depending on size, blanch four to eight outside cabbage leaves. Divide the meat mixture equally among them. Wrap and tie; I use ordinary button thread. Simmer slowly for an hour or more in tomato sauce.

A quarter pound of hamburger will turn an eggplant or zucchini casserole into a tasty and filling main dish. Both are made by browning slices of the vegetable, layering it alternately with onions and sliced or grated cheese, pouring tomato sauce over all and topping with flavored bread crumbs. Sometimes I dice the eggplant or cut it into julienne strips. If you are generous with the cheese, this can be your piece de resistance as is, but adding the quarter pound of hamburger gives it a real "main dish" flavor. I have carried these dishes—both with and without the meat—to covered dish suppers and always had them well received.

Another recipe which can be turned into a main dish with the addition of just a bit of meat is scalloped potatoes. Top them with thin slices of Canadian bacon or sausage, or split links of sausage or halves of hot dogs. I sometimes alternate the layers of potato with thin slices of ham, or stir slivers of ham into the white sauce.

Put leftover ham through the meat grinder with onion and day old bread and you have the basis for a ham loaf, patties or croquettes. Or omit the bread and mash the ham-onion mixture into egg yolks for ham-deviled eggs. These are good served warm with a cream gravy over them.

Bits of any meat can be stirred into an omelet. To many people, a plain omelet is an acceptable meat substitute, since eggs are a good source of protein. Two of my children were very negative about eggs, but I serve them more often now that my husband and I are alone. Usually I begin by frying onion. Sometimes I add bits of green pepper and pimento, especially if I do not include any meat, and often top it with a mushroom or cheese sauce.

My daughter makes a main dish omelet that begins with frying a sliced garlic bud in olive oil. After the garlic is removed, thin sliced onions and potatoes are sauteed in the oil before the beaten eggs are poured in. This is another dish she learned in Spain and it is very satisfying.

Hot dogs are a very economical meat buy which should not be overlooked. They do not always have to be served inside a roll. Topped with a tangy mustard sauce, they provide a sufficient meat serving with a baked potato—either white or sweet. Sausage also goes well with baked potatoes. Hot dogs can be sliced into omelets or into a casserole of lentils before serving. Split lengthwise, they make an attractive topping for homemade baked beans or for any otherwise meatless casserole.

One of my favorite uses for the last bits of a piece

of beef or pork is to make chop suey. The meat is especially good marinated in soy sauce. A can of bean sprouts forms the basis for the dish. You need only thicken the water they are packed in with cornstarch, add a teaspoon of molasses if you have it, and soy sauce to taste.

Just a few minutes before serving, add strips of green and/or red peppers and onions—purple ones make it attractive—and the meat. A great deal of variation is possible: celery can be added, bits of pimento, slices of mushroom, a few sliced water chestnuts, if you have them. Chop suey can be dressed up by using pineapple juice for part of the liquid and adding a few almonds.

Once when I did not have a can of bean sprouts and did have a large picking of Swiss chard, I discovered that the stems of the chard made an excellent substitute when split lengthwise into thirds. If this dish is served with rice, it is chop suey. If served with Chinese noodles, which makes it more expensive, it is chow mein.

With the remains of a lamb roast I prefer to make curry because it is one of my husband's favorite dishes. However, because the children were not fond of it, I have not made it frequently enough to do much experimenting—merely following the recipe on the box of curry powder or one from a cookbook.

When you are hunting for a bargain, do not overlook the fact that many stores sell the tag ends of their delicatessen meats at greatly reduced prices. If you select them carefully, you can get a real bonus. There will be some slices—ragged-looking to be sure, but no different in taste—suitable for sandwiches, and frequently the thick heel of the loaf of meat.

These ends can be ground for spreads or used in some of the dinner dishes suggested. Beef, for instance, can be cut small for chop suey. Bologna substitutes for any of the ham or hot dog suggestions. Sometimes you will be fortunate enough to find a package that contains nothing but boiled ham.

We have one favorite summer night dinner that is strictly for two; the children did not find it filling enough. Basically, it is a lettuce bowl to which I add whatever other vegetables are on hand or in the garden—radishes, celery, onions, pepper, tomatoes, grated carrot, leftover green beans, young beet or chard leaves, parsley—plus bits of ham, chicken, cheese, and sometimes homemade seasoned croutons. Our first choice of dressing is blue cheese, but others can be used according to one's individual taste. All we have with this are hot rolls or homemade bread, and dessert. We find this dinner both delicious and satisfying. It is also economical since I grow most of the vegetables and save bits of ham and chicken in the freezer for such a use.

Until a few years ago, we enjoyed fresh and frozen fish as a good budget-balancer, but more recently fish has been priced to keep company with steak, at least in our area.

If you have used up this month's quota of meat and you have already served macaroni and cheese a sufficient number of times, you can still pull a new trick out of the oven. My husband told me to be sure to share this one with you.

Slice a large onion or two into margarine or bacon grease and saute gently until limp. Add about three quarters cup of milk, as much grated cheese as you like, and salt and pepper to taste. The cheese can be any kind you have on hand, or a combination if you are down to odds and ends. The stronger the cheese flavor, the better the dish.

Beat thoroughly two to four eggs. Four is best, but if you are short, you can use fewer and increase the milk a little. If you can't spare eggs at all, substitute white sauce. The dish will still be tasty but you will have lost protein value. Stir the first mixture until the cheese melts, but do not let the milk boil. Slowly add the hot milk about a tablespoon at a time as you continue beating the eggs.

By the time you have used about half the liquid, you can pour the egg mixture into the pan as you continue to stir. By introducing the hot liquid slowly into the eggs, you avoid having them set. Most experienced cooks know this but young brides sometimes have to learn it the hard way. After it has all been combined, pour into a pie shell and top with more cheese. Bake at about 375° until set and serve as your main dish along with some colorful vegetables.

We do like good steaks and chops; we always consider them a treat. But I honestly feel sorry for those who consider them necessary on a daily basis. Even if economy is not their problem, they miss so much by not discovering the interest and variety that is possible from many humble dishes.

*LOVE IS Jelly on the Bread*

# 10
# All Our Needs

*If thou of fortune be bereft*
*And in thy store there be but left*
*Two loaves, sell one and with the dole*
*Buy hyacinths to feed thy soul.*
James Terry White

The author of these lines was echoing an old Persian philosophy that a man who had only a dime should spend a nickel for a loaf of bread and a nickel for a pot of hyacinths. Today, of course, one would need several dimes for either the bread or the flowers, but the point is still valid. Our basic needs are not satisfied merely with that which assures our physical survival.

We have a God who has promised to supply all our needs. Now, admittedly, in the context of Philippians 4:19, Paul is talking about material needs. The church at Philippi was not going to suffer any lack because they had been generous in their offering to the Apostle. But we are safe in suggesting that the God who will not let us lack bread will also see to it that those "hyacinth" needs of the soul He created in us will likewise be taken care of. Even amid the humdrum of our daily concern with the physical needs of home and family, we can take time to be aware of His greater provision.

Have you stopped to admire or to show your children how many shades of green can be discerned in one salad bowl? Or taken time to enjoy the rich redness of a tomato on a bed of greens? The Creator could have made just one kind of plant dedicated to the production of multi-vitamin capsules mixed with proper proportions of protein; instead, He chose to sustain us through the delight of taste, the beauty of color, the excitement of texture. His provision includes satisfaction of our need for companionship—the joy of family and friends sharing His bounty around a table. Man seems always to have recognized that the act of eating is a social as well as a physical fulfillment, and the preparation of food is a service that recognizes and expresses our relationships and affections.

His supplies are neither stinting nor grudging but "... exceeding abundantly above all that we can ask or think ..." (Ephesians 3:20). The sun which must warm and energize us also paints with glorious color on the sky. The food which must sustain us delights our eyes and taste at the same time. And best of all is the privilege of sharing His bounty and His beauty with those whose care He has entrusted to us.

*To meditate on: Am I so busy caring for the bodies of my family that their souls are undernourished? Dear Lord, keep me aware of Your hyacinths that I may not fail to take time to discover and share them with those You have given to me.*

*LOVE IS Jelly on the Bread*

# 11
# Variety with Vegetables

How our Lord must have enjoyed creating vegetables. He could so easily have crammed all our necessary vitamins and minerals into one kind of bean or squash, but He didn't. Perhaps nowhere in nature has He treated us with such an exuberant variety of texture, color and flavor as is available in our edible vegetables. Yet, probably nothing we eat is treated with more indifference and even disdain—from Dennis the Menace rebelling against a serving of carrots to the expensive restaurant that serves up perfectly prepared prime ribs or seafood and dumps beside them a tired spoonful of watery, unflavored peas or beans.

In contrast, I remember with real pleasure a luncheon affair I attended at a modest cost where I was warmed at the sight of the food before I took the first bite. A piece of chicken rested on a tasty mound of stuffing, but the bright beauty of the plate came from a trio of vegetables. Beside a nice serving of frenched green beans was an offering of well-flavored carrots cut somewhat on a bias. Beside these was a single circle of pickled red beet slice nestling on a small pillow of curly endive.

Whoever prepared those plates had the soul of an artist, but he did not do anything that we cannot all do at home to brighten the table and excite the appetites of our families.

If you, like us, rely on a garden and also keep alert for opportunities to make large purchases at small cost, there are times when you find yourself with an abundance of a single vegetable. This does not have to be boring if you make yourself aware of the many possible ways in which one vegetable can be prepared.

Because our small plot produces at one season an abundance of snap beans, and just a little later an equal abundance of zucchini, I have on my cookbook shelf, file folders filled with clippings of ways to prepare each of these.

If you have a garden surplus of peppers or find a good buy at your produce stand, by all means freeze some. Although they will not be crisp enough to use in salads after freezing, they are great for any cooked dish. Just browsing through a cookbook will reward you with new ideas for any quantity of food you may have on hand. Paging through an old, familiar cookbook is never a wasted pastime for anyone faced with preparing three meals a day for a third of a century. No less a food expert than James Beard advises, "There is such a wealth of ideas in good cookbooks that no one can collect all of them in a lifetime."

I recall a number of occasions when I have had to present the same vegetable over a period of many days, but perhaps I can illustrate with two incidents—one from the first year of our marriage, and one from just recently.

We were living in Chicago where my husband was a graduate student and our budget was slim. My culinary experience was minimal and my eagerness to be cooperative maximal. Late one Saturday afternoon a truck farmer, driving through the city streets eager to dispose of his last remaining produce, offered me a large carton of celery for a quarter. I took it.

The first thing I had to learn, of course, was how to keep celery fresh. (You cut off the ends of the stalks and stand them in water in the refrigerator.) It was a lot of celery; we tended to avoid it for awhile afterward. But by having it I learned to achieve some variety. I served it in the usual ways—as is, spread with cheese, cut up in tossed salads. We discovered that it added a pleasant crunchiness when cooked with other vegetables.

I learned to make cream of celery soup, as well as a celeried white sauce for casseroles. The leafy portions made a good addition to soup stock which was made from meat or poultry bones. It is delicious in stuffing, to which it can be added generously. Braised celery is also a good and different vegetable. None of this involved originality on my part; it was just a matter of doing some recipe research.

The more recent experience we owe to a friend who planted a field of beets because he hated to see the land going to waste. We thoroughly appreciated a few bunches he presented to us, so when he finished his harvesting he gave us two full cartons of them! Some were so huge that a single beet would serve eight or more. Happily, beets keep well, and it is always delightful to have something you can share with friends. They can also be frozen. I fell into the routine of preparing twice as much as I needed for a given meal and putting half into the freezer. And I pickled several quarts.

But that still left a lot of beets. I have put them on the table as buttered beets, harvard beets, beets with orange and/or onion, jellied beet salad, marinated beets and baked beets. A nice way to use leftover cooked ones is to cut them up, and toss with a little green pepper, onion and cubes of cheese and serve on a bed of lettuce.

The baked beet idea was a tip from a friend: A beet the right size for an individual serving, or for two servings when cut in half, can be wrapped in foil, baked, and served like a sweet potato with salt, pepper and margarine. These are delicious. Even the foil is not necessary, but without it the leaf end has a rather charred look.

Beets, by the way, should be cooked whole to prevent bleeding out of the color. To prepare the various recipes above, I first boil them whole, then peel and cut them for their intended use.

Variety can also be attained just by changing the shape in which food is served from day to day. The beets, for example, can be sliced, cubed, or cut julienne style. The smaller ones are attractive when served whole. Nor should the leafy tops be neglected. Unless they are quite old and ragged they can be cooked and flavored like any green, and served with the beets — sometimes as a bed under them. The youngest, tenderest leaves can be mixed raw with lettuce in a tossed salad bowl.

Your items of abundance may be entirely different. Cabbage or carrots are often the best vegetable buys in the market. At some seasons so is squash. If you have a garden you may, in years of early frost, rescue many green tomatoes. These can be made into pickles and relish. They are also good sliced thick, dipped in batter and fried.

Just recently, when I had a large quantity of broccoli, I discovered that I could slice the heavy stem ends into circlets and use them as I would zucchini— in a casserole, or fried with onions with or without tomato sauce added. George said, "This is good; it should be in your book."

Another way to serve gourmet vegetables with economy is to spend a few minutes doing research at your grocer's frozen food section. Find the packages of ridiculously expensive, prepared vegetables. Study the pictures, read the lists of ingredients and the serving suggestions. Then buy packages of plain frozen vegetables, or some fresh ones, and go and do likewise.

Regardless of whether you must major on it for a period of time without becoming tired of it, or want to be sure it complements whatever else you are serving in color, texture, shape and flavor, no vegetable has to become boring. The Creator made vegetables beautiful; we can rise to the challenge of serving them beautifully.

# 12
# Vitamin B Complex

It is a rare homemaker who is not aware of the important part that vitamins play in the nourishment of her family. She may not be sure of exactly what the various A, B, C, D, E and others do for them, but she does know they are needed.

Among the most basic of these are the B vitamins found abundantly in our grain and "staff of life" foods, bread and cereal. It should not surprise us, therefore, to find that the Word of God which should be our daily spiritual bread is also abundantly supplied with B vitamins.

"Be strong" (Ephesians 6:10b), not in ourselves, but in the Lord. There is no healthy or abundant life apart from Him. "Be ... kind" (Ephesians 4:32a). Without this important vitamin, our interrelationships, even as Christians, will be at best anemic and sickly.

"Be of good cheer" (John 16:33c). This is only possible in every circumstance if we believe that "All things work together for good to them that love God" (Romans 8:28a). Solomon said, "A merry heart doeth good like a medicine" (Proverbs 17:22a). Vitamins are as important to our spiritual well-being as to the physical.

A subgroup of these important vitamins are the "be nots." "Be not afraid" (I Peter 3:14b); "be not conformed" (Romans 12:2a); and "be . . . not un-equally yoked" (II Corinthians 6:14) are among the most vital. There can be no robust spiritual life where these vitamins are lacking.

*To meditate on: Am I assimilating sufficient Bible vitamins to be spiritually robust for the task of leading my family? Dear Lord, show me how I and those for whom I am responsible can be sure of a vitamin-packed diet from our daily meals at Your table.*

*LOVE IS Jelly on the Bread*

# 13
# A Bountiful
# Bread Box

The good Lord probably does not intend His children to enjoy perfect contentment on this earth. If we were perfectly content, we would forget to desire His presence and His house. But He does sometimes give us a taste of pure contentment, perhaps in order that we may anticipate what the complete and eternal contentment of His Presence will be.

At least three things in my experience have given that foretaste of contentment. One is nursing a baby. Another is emerging mentally wrung out from concentration on a piece of writing knowing it is GOOD (admittedly too rare a finale). The third is baking a beautiful batch of bread. In this case, the contentment begins with the act of kneading, grows as the aroma of rising and baking dough permeates the atmosphere, and climaxes with the contemplation of a perfect product.

Since I claim no knowledge of psychology, I do not attempt to explain such satisfaction. I do know, however, that there is a contentment of body produced by good bread that encompasses those who eat as well as those who cook. Perhaps more than anything else on a menu, it provides the satisfaction and staying power that comes with knowing you have had enough.

It is not for nothing that bread has been called the staff of life. In every culture the staple of the people's diet is a grain product, without which they starve. The children of Israel needed bread from Heaven to sustain them in the wilderness, even though they must also have utilized milk and cheese from their cattle.

Much has been made in Bible teaching and preaching about the Israelites longing after the leeks and garlic of Egypt — the vegetables they were accustomed to eating. But in Exodus 16:3 it was the bread they formerly could eat to the full that was causing their hunger unto death in the wilderness. Even though they must have had the milk and cheese from their cattle as they journeyed, they could not live without grains, which they could not tarry in any place long enough to produce. God graciously met this great need for His wandering people by sending them bread from Heaven.

When Joseph was in Egypt, his relatives in Canaan were in danger of starving without his grain even though they had fruit, nuts and honey, as well as cattle (Genesis 43:11).

A simple soup or salad dinner becomes a feast when the right bread is served with it. My favorites are an onion and a cheese bread. Others I like to bake on occasion are tomato, oatmeal, orange, molasses and cinnamon. A bit of browsing through the bread chapter of your cookbook will acquaint you with a tempting variety.

Since many standard recipes make two loaves or two dozen rolls, you can freeze half your production and, within a short time, be able to serve an assortment of breads on a few minutes notice.

It is admittedly somewhat time-consuming to make yeast breads, but it is not difficult as long as one remembers to treat the yeast with respect. I prefer to use the powdered variety because it keeps a long time and is easier to handle than the cakes. By buying yeast in a jar rather than in individual packages it is very economical.

The liquid used in the recipe must be warm enough to encourage growth of the yeast, but not so hot as to kill it. Most directions call for scalding the liquid, then letting it cool down. Shake a few drops on your wrist as you would a baby formula; it should feel warm but not hot.

Yeast also likes a warm, draft-free environment in which to do its job of raising the dough. The bowl should be thoroughly warmed before placing the dough in it. A chilly bowl can prolong the rising process. The time of year and the temperature of your house will usually dictate the best place to put the dough. I have a friend who likes to set hers in a closed car with the sun beating down on it. Some cookbooks suggest putting it in an unlighted oven with a large pan of boiling water on the lower shelf. This often works very well, but it works even better if another pan of boiling water is set on top of the bowl.

I have also found it effective to set the dough on top of the stove over the pilot with an asbestos pad under the bowl and a pan of boiling water resting on top of it. Over all that, I invert a large, round roasting pan which has been rinsed with hot water.

Usually the rising will be complete within the time specified by the recipe, but if it is not, that is no cause for discouragement. Just replace the boiling water and make sure you have chosen the warmest possible spot.

I have never known a batch not to rise eventually. Once I gave up on a batch and went off to bed in disgust, leaving the bowl of dough sitting on the stove. When I came down in the morning, it had risen beautifully.

Yeast bread is not really more time-consuming to make than quick breads. It is the necessity of catching it for the next step when it has had the right amount of rising time that makes it seem so. Most recipes call for two risings. For this reason, it may not always be feasible for a working person to fit yeast breadmaking into her schedule. I do not try to make yeast bread when I am pushing a deadline.

There are, however, many quick breads which are equally effective for adding variety and interest to your meals. An ordinary baking powder biscuit recipe is capable of a number of variations. Cheese, bacon, ham, onion, herb, orange, or cinnamon biscuits are just a few.

With only a few minutes' effort, even store-bought bread can be made exciting. Here is one method my family particularly enjoys. Slice a loaf of French or Italian bread almost all the way through. Soften a stick of margarine, mix with garlic salt or powder to taste, and spread on the slices and over the top of the loaf. Wrap tightly in foil and heat in the oven.

Even an ordinary loaf of sliced white bread can be handled this way. Here are some other possible flavor combinations. In each case the ingredients are mixed into the softened butter or margarine:

Grated cheese, any flavor
Onion salt and parsley flakes
Ketchup and oregano, with or without grated Italian cheese
Sugar and cinnamon mixture
Sugar and grated orange rind, with a few drops of orange juice

Your own imagination and knowledge of your family's flavor preferences will soon suggest others to you.

If you have trouble getting members of your family to eat a proper breakfast, do not overlook bread as a valuable ally. Few people can resist the lure of fresh yeast rolls, muffins or coffee cakes. Since many recipes call for eggs, milk, cereal, even fruits and nuts, they make a nourishing as well as pleasant start for the day.

Finally, if you live near a bakery, or if your grocer keeps a rack for marked down bread products, keep track of it. It is another way of getting a variety in baked goods at real economy. Monday morning is an especially good time for such buys if your grocer is closed on Sunday. Unfortunately, in our part of the country at least, Sunday closings are becoming the exception.

Bread is a basic food important to our well-being. It can be prepared and served in a manner that shows recognition of its value.

# 14
# Sweet Tooth

Jeremiah said it so beautifully. Whenever I see or hear his words, I get a tingle up my spine. "Thy words were found, and I did eat them; and thy word was unto me the joy and rejoicing of mine heart: for I am called by thy name, O Lord God of hosts" (Jeremiah 15:16).

Someone has said there are three ways to "eat" God's Word: as medicine — unpleasant but necessary; as shredded wheat — dry but nourishing; or as strawberry shortcake. Obviously, the last is what Jeremiah had discovered the Word to be. David also testified that the Word of God brought complete satisfaction to his spiritual sweet tooth; he found it "sweeter also than honey and the honeycomb" (Psalm 19:10b).

The God who created us with a sweet tooth and filled the earth with the fruits, honeys, sugar canes and maple saps that would satisfy it knows well how to provide His children with the right amount of sweetness in their spiritual diet — that which satisfies without being cloying or debilitating. Just as a diet of desserts would make us flabby, if not ill, so the food of the Heavenly family is perfectly proportioned.

To build good spiritual muscle, we need the strong meat of doctrine and the vegetables of rebuke, reproof and correction, but we also need that final touch of sweetness that says, "I love you and want you to leave My table both with what you need and with what will leave you feeling satisfied and content. My food is both healthy and pleasant."

What are His sweet portions? Might they not include the paeans of praise that remind us what a great God we have, the precious promises that assure us of His watchful care and attention to our needs, the many passages that tell us how truly we are loved, the foreglimpses of what awaits us at home in our Father's house? Is it not all sweetness when we recognize that even those portions that taste like medicine, or require much chewing, or contain rebukes difficult to digest, are served out of a wise and abundant love that envisions us as mature sons and daughters sound and beautiful in heart and mind and spirit?

*To meditate on: Am I too often guilty of serving God's Word to my family like a dose of medicine meant to cure their spiritual ailments? Dear Lord, help me to keep their diet in balance and share with them also the sweetness I have enjoyed at Your table.*

*LOVE IS Jelly on the Bread*

# 15
# The Sweet Finale

Since I have been working on these chapters, my mammoth refrigerator-freezer has given up and died, worn out from its twenty years of very active service. Because economic realities plus our decreased family size dictated that it be replaced by a significantly smaller model, some changes in our lifestyle have become necessary. Not the least of these changes pertains to the question of desserts.

Ice cream has always been our favorite. Compared to other desserts, it is relatively inexpensive when purchased by the half gallon, especially under local supermarket brand names. Even the leading brands frequently have sales or coupon offers that bring their prices down to the market brand level.

Ice cream is easily and quickly served when lack of time prohibits preparing something else, or when unexpected company arrives. With its many flavors, there is one kind to please every taste. It is the perfect solution when another dessert, such as fresh fruit, cake, and many kinds of pie, needs to be stretched.

For years it has been my practice to keep at least

half a dozen packages on hand. This was the first thing that had to change with the new appliance. The alternative was to cease freezing homegrown vegetables, and I fear that must be somewhat curtailed in any case.

For everyday family meals, my desserts have always been simple. I make use of seasonal fruits, served fresh or in suitable recipes. For example, when the apple tree is producing, we have several weeks of pies, brown Bettys, cobblers, and similar favorites. When oranges are inexpensive, I like to use a delicious but absurdly simple dessert my daughter learned during her European residence. The oranges are peeled, sliced and heavily sprinkled with cinnamon. If this is done a couple of hours before serving, they are even better.

Packaged puddings and gelatins are always a favorite with children and can be easily and quickly prepared. Fruit may be added. Puddings have the advantage of adding extra milk to the diet. A small dab of packaged whip on each serving does not add significantly to the cost, but does a great deal for the eye appeal. Other ways of improving the appearance of puddings: sprinkle them with colored sugar, cinnamon or nutmeg, or chopped nuts; center with a cherry, large berry, or half nut meat.

For a variation that requires little effort, combine two or more colors of pudding in parfait glasses. Or alternate pudding with one or more of the following in contrasting colors: Jello, ice cream, whipped cream, fruit or fruit sauces. With a little thought, you can tickle your family by serving a dessert color-keyed to a particular holiday.

Cookies have been another of our most common

family desserts because my husband has always wanted some on hand for late night snacks. The day I bake the cookies, they are the dessert.

Even candy is an acceptable finale. I have never been a candy buyer or maker, and have always discouraged the children from eating it for snacks, but occasionally, there would be a gift box in the house. When passed around the table for the final course, it was received with unanimous pleasure.

Frequently, too, I have occasion to provide pie, cake or brownies for covered dish meals. At such times, I make enough to also serve the family for the next two or three days. Otherwise, although I dearly love a properly moist and rich cake, I have generally limited them to birthdays because my experience has been that the really good ones are expensive and time-consuming. I use mixes only for an emergency or when the cake is a mere auxiliary and not the star.

One of my boys made it clear before he was ten that he considered birthday cakes an unnecessary tradition, and that it would be a great improvement if people would put the candles on a pie. He has had a birthday pie ever since, usually apple because that is his favorite. Besides, his birthday is in the fall!

He is happy with any apple pie, but his number one favorite is a kind of open-faced tart. Years ago I clipped the recipe from a magazine and subsequently lost it, but still make what I think is a reasonable facsimile. One layer of sliced apples is spread over the bottom crust. Top it with your favorite combination of white and/or brown sugar, spices and thickening. I prefer using tapioca as a thickener instead of flour with my fruit pies.

Pare and core four additional apples and cut them

in half crosswise. Arrange these cut side down on top of the sliced layer and top with the remainder of the sugar-spice-thickening mixture. Carefully pour about a quarter cup of evaporated milk around the edges of the pie, dot with butter, and bake.

One personal idiosyncrasy is that, whenever possible, I avoid the use of a top crust. If I have one at all, it is in the form of lattices or suitable shapes cut with cookie cutters or shaped by hand — bells for Christmas, bunnies or tulips for Easter, hatchets for a Washington's birthday cherry pie. The possibilities are endless. More often, however, I make a streusel topping, adding ground or chopped nuts if the occasion is special; or a glazed topping from homemade jelly, of which I usually have a suitable complementary flavor on the shelf.

I have a brownies specialty for which I am often asked the recipe, although it is ridiculously simple. Make up an ordinary chocolate chip cookie recipe, but spread it in a baking pan rather than dropping it onto a cookie sheet. It is best made with chopped nuts and raisins, but an economy version that substitutes two cups of Rice Krispies has proven equally popular. I usually top this with chocolate fudge or coffee icing before cutting into squares.

Chocolate chips seem to be almost everyone's favorite, but I prefer using butterscotch chips for these brownies. When I do, I use golden rather than dark raisins and make a caramel icing. Another variation uses lemon chips. Since these are not as readily available in the stores, I have done it only a few times. With lemon chips, I use all white sugar to keep the brownie light in color, golden raisins, and a lemon frosting.

Company meals call for the dessert to be a little more elaborate unless the main course itself is unusually elaborate or time-consuming to prepare. In the latter event I stick to ice cream, either with a topping of fruit or sauce with whipped cream, or served in an assortment of color combinations. Otherwise, on company occasions I may make one of my fancier cakes or pies, or a special seasonal favorite such as strawberry shortcake — preferably the old-fashioned biscuit dough kind. When I really want to produce spontaneous exclamations of surprise and delight, my choice is Baked Alaska. In spite of its effect on the recipients — I find many people have never even heard of it — this dessert is surprisingly simple to make and capable of almost unlimited variations.

I first discovered Baked Alaska when my children were infants. I do not know what current medical theory is, but at that time I was told babies needed an egg yolk a day until they were a year old, but no whites because they might make them subject to allergies. So egg whites accumulated rather fast in the refrigerator. When I got tired of making angel food cake, I began researching other uses for the whites with the result that, with much fear and trembling, I made my first Baked Alaska. It was an immediate hit.

Basically, this dish consists of a block of very firm ice cream resting on a layer of cake and covered with meringue. The ice cream must be placed so the cake base extends at least half an inch beyond it on all sides, and the meringue must completely cover the ice cream to the borders of the base. Then it is baked about four minutes in a very hot oven until the meringue has turned the desired shade of brown. The ice cream does not melt because the cake and egg white serve as insulation. For further protection, a layer of brown paper should be placed between the baking sheet and the cake.

Any kind of cake works well in this recipe. It should be chosen to complement the flavor of ice cream used. My family's favorite is a chocolate brownie mix for the base. Pie crust is another good base, graham cracker or cookie crumb being particularly suitable. A fruit pie becomes something glamorous if you put just one layer of fruit in your crust then, after it is baked, fill the remainder with ice cream which can, if desired, be heaped to mound higher than the pie-plate. Cover it with foil and put it in the freezer overnight to insure that the ice cream is very hard. When ready to serve, spread on the meringue, being careful to seal it to the edges of the crust, and brown.

Many desserts and other recipes containing eggs call for separating eggs and beating the whites very stiff. In order to get stiff whites it is important not to have even a drop of the yolk in them. Recipes do not always bother to explain that eggs separate more efficiently when cold, but the whites beat up fuller when at room temperature; but it is important to know. I take my eggs out an hour or so before I intend to use them and separate them immediately. Then I leave the bowl of whites sitting out until I am ready to beat them. If the recipe calls for beating both whites and yolks and you are using the same beaters, do the whites *first.* If a drop of yolk gets into the whites as they are being separated it can often be cleanly removed by using one of the shell halves as a scoop.

Beaters containing dried egg or batter or potato (I like to mash mine with a mixer) are a headache to clean. It can be avoided just by putting them to soak in the pans or bowls right after using. In the case of eggs use cold water for the soaking.

A bride who borrowed a cake recipe from me asked why she had trouble getting it from the pans. "Did you grease them?" I asked. "Oh, yes," she assured me.

"Did you sift a light dusting of flour over the grease?" I continued. No, that had not occurred to her. Later she informed me that added tip made the difference, but she had never heard of it before.

Desserts, properly planned, are not a mere appendix to a meal, but an integral part of your nutritional plan. If your dinner has a minimum of protein, an egg or milk dessert increases it. If the main course seems a little light, one of the heavier desserts completes it in satisfying fashion. Almost every meal seems better for having the right sweet touch at the end. Like the jelly on the toast, the dessert has a way of saying, "I love you," to the family. And to your guests, "I'm awfully glad you came."

# 16
# The Better Part
# of Hostessing

I have a very great fondness for Martha (Luke 10:38ff). I rather strongly suspect that the reason she lost her cool was that she envied Mary. She too, wanted to be in the living room, listening to the wonderful conversation of the Saviour. Being conscientious, however, and loving Him as she did, she must have felt that only her very best and most elaborate dinner properly expressed her appreication for having Him under her roof.

If you have ever struggled to keep half a dozen or more last minute details in proper balance while sounds of enthusiastic discussion or peals of laughter drifted out to you from the living room, you will appreciate exactly what Martha must have been feeling.

It was no light thing to serve dinner to a dozen hungry men, and Martha surely thought she was giving her very best for the Master and His companions. Just as certainly, Jesus must have expressed warm appreciation for the lovely dinner before He left her home.

If Martha had only realized that providing food is just half of good hostessing! The other half, which

Mary recognized, is showing real pleasure in the company of and fellowship with the guest. Martha could have learned to plan worthy meals which were prepared before the guests arrived and, thereby, she would have been free to tune in on much more of the wonderful conversation. She also, no doubt, would have kept her disposition intact!

Over and over the New Testament exalts hospitality as a Christian virtue. It is one of the necessary requirements for those who aspire to leadership in the church (I Timothy 3:2). But, to be specifically Christian, such hospitality must go beyond the sharing of fellowship with family and friends. It requires opening one's home to the Lord's servants (Romans 12:13; III John 6-9) and to the stranger, especially the needy and lonely (Hebrews 13:2).

No other Christian responsibility is more rewarding, for the blessings that revert to the hostess and her household are far more abundant than those she bestows. Her circle of friends is enlarged, her vision of the mission fields and other ministries is enhanced, and her appreciation of other lives and cultures is enriched. Best of all, she sees the same cultural enrichment taking place in her children, along with their ability to entertain others, appreciate their conversation, and make them feel at home.

The Gospels show that Jesus Himself was often a guest. His hosts included not only Martha who fretted over the responsibility, but a Pharisee who neglected the common courtesies, a disciple who was eager to introduce his friends to the Saviour, a rich publican, and a couple mourning His death.

But Jesus also made opportunities to be a host.

The Gospels describe three such occasions in addition to the Passover supper. He once fed five thousand, at another time four thousand, and once prepared breakfast for His disciples. In each of these three instances His menu was simple — bread and fish — but the fellowship and concern for His guests' well-being made the occasions unforgettable.

Today He asks us to become His host: "Behold, I stand at the door, and knock: if any man hear my voice, and open the door, I will come in to him, and will sup with him, and he with me" (Revelation 3:20). Tomorrow He wants to become our host: "Blessed are they which are called unto the marriage supper of the Lamb" (Revelation 19:9b).

*To meditate on: Is my home a center of Christian hospitality where guests are welcome for the Lord's sake and not only because they are people I enjoy? Dear Lord, make me fruitful in this area of Christian responsibility.*

# 17
# Company Coming?
# It Needn't
# Be Steak

Among my very pleasant memories of the earliest years of our marriage are the Saturday evenings we spent together with four or five other young couples over a dinner of waffles, hot dogs, scrambled eggs or chili. Each hostess had her specialty. It was shortly after World War II and all the husbands were university students supported by the GI Bill, while all the wives had at least part-time jobs to eke out the living allowance. The minimum hourly wage at that time was fifty cents.

During those same years, however, if my pastor or in-laws, or anyone else on whom I wanted to make a proper impression came to dinner, I was afraid to serve them anything less than steak. Needless to say, the pleasure of the company was somewhat mitigated by the subsequent problem of unsnarling the grocery budget.

Now, more than thirty years later, I still love entertaining but I do not like eating soup for a week thereafter. Furthermore, I have learned that people do not expect steak dinners, but often remember with pleasure an everyday entree served in a little different way or accompanied by an unusual vegetable or dessert.

At a fun dinner I attended some time ago, the menu consisted of a bowl of beef cut into very small cubes, a large tossed salad, an assortment of tasty breads, plus cookies and good hot coffee. The meat cubes were speared and dipped into one of two fondue pots containing different sauces. A little meat took a long time to eat this way and instigated much good fellowship. I do not have a fondue pot but have been tempted ever since to get one.

I believe the cubes for that meal were cut from a piece of boneless sirloin, for they were very tender. It is one way of using the best beef and stretching it. My own favorite method for stretching good beef is to make stroganoff. With one pound of good boneless round and a four-ounce can of mushroom stems and pieces, I can serve eight, and stroganoff seems to be universally popular.

Other cuts of beef also produce first-rate meals. If pot roasts are on special the week you are expecting guests, consider yourself fortunate. My favorite recipe calls for oven-roasting one in a covered pan. If you do not have a covered pan, you can use aluminum foil, but that makes it more expensive. A large covered roasting pan is worth having. I only regret that mine will not hold a turkey of more than twelve pounds as they are far more moist and delicious when covered while cooking.

For the pot roast, brown some thick slices of onion in a pan. Sprinkle the meat with flour and an envelope of powdered onion or mushroom soup mix, shake Worcestershire sauce over the surface, and salt and pepper to taste. When I have green pepper I also like to lay pieces of it over the meat. It adds a bright freshness of taste even though the color fades somewhat during cooking. A small can of mushroom pieces adds the final touch to your roast. If you do not use the mushrooms you will need to add a little water, which should not reach higher than the surface of the meat trivet.

Finally, add a sufficient number of small to medium peeled potatoes. They will be deliciously brown and tender when served. Depending on the size of your roast, cooking will take from one to two hours in an oven of about 350 degrees. Frequently, I put this dish in the oven just before leaving for Sunday School and it is ready when we return from church. I have never found it necessary, nor thought it right, to stay home on Sunday because guests were expected.

When you are ready to serve this roast, slice it onto a warm platter and pour the sauce over it, thickened with a little flour, or cornstarch if you prefer. Brighten the platter with a bit of parsley, pickled crab apple, or other favorite colorful garnish.

Even the lowly hamburger is not to be scorned as a company dish. I have often served spaghetti with meat sauce or Swedish meat balls. Chili is another favorite if I am sure about the tastes of my guests. Recently at a book discussion we were served stroganoff made with hamburger that produced raves from everyone present. I have another friend who makes a lasagna that people invariably look forward to.

If you browse through a collection of meat loaf and meatball recipes, you will come up with a number of other good-enough-for-company dishes. Chicken is always a good buy, usually a favorite, and the number of ways it can be prepared is almost endless. Barbequed chicken is universally popular and every standard cookbook will include one or more recipes for it. Even a very simple dinner can seem festive if served with an attractive appetizer and dessert.

A little attention to the right choice of tableware can help to make your guests feel honored. My own prized possession is a set of hand-painted bouillon cups that had been in my husband's family for years. I often serve a light soup as the first course just as a reason to use them!

Another attractive way to begin a meal is with a seasonal fruit cup. It has an advantage also in that it can be prepared ahead and served with little difficulty if your entree is one that takes last minute attention.

Fruit in season is, in fact, a versatile and relatively inexpensive dish for either end of the meal. It is always popular spooned over ice cream with a dollup of whip if desired. It can be served whole with an assortment of cheeses. Your wedding present bowl or silver tray will come into its own with this one.

By all means, honor your company with the best you can, and by no means apologize for it. If it is well cooked, beautifully presented, and — most importantly—served with good conversation and genuine pleasure, your evening will be a success for both guests and hostess.

# 18
# Thanksgiving

A checkout girl remarked that almost everyone who went through her counter made some complaint about the high cost of food. as if she were personally responsible. I am sure she was not exaggerating; I know I have been guilty of it. Why is it we are not as quick to be thankful that we are still able to buy a sufficient amount of food?

In the first chapter of Romans we are told something both significant and practical about man's separation from God. "When they knew God, they glorified him not as God, neither were thankful" (verse 21). The first step man takes into sin is failure to glorify the Lord, and the second is ingratitude. What a terribly common and everyday sin it is!

Isn't it lack of a thankful spirit that crabs our dispositions and sours our personal relationships? Isn't thanklessness at the root of covetousness, envy, faultfinding, grumbling and feeling sorry for oneself? How easy it is to count the other fellow's blessings instead of our own! Our Heavenly Father is much wiser than we human parents who so often try to treat all our children exactly alike, lest they accuse us of favoring one over the other. He treats us as individuals, giving to each one exactly the blessing best suited to our individual need and not necessarily the one He has given our brother.

Sometimes we remember to express thanks for the big blessings—a good husband, a new baby, a grown-up child who can be viewed with pride, a nice raise or promotion. Then, we take for granted the small and daily joys—the call or note from a friend, the beauty in commonplace things, the supply of everyday needs. Yet, a thankful awareness of these things doubles the pleasure they bring.

Every good gift, no matter what its immediate source, comes to us from the hand of our Heavenly Father (James 1:17). The following three chapters of this book are my thanksgiving for seemingly small, daily benefits with which God overwhelms me; for having that which I can give away, and for the ability to provide touches of love with even minimal outlays of time or money.

*To meditate on: Do I take for granted those daily blessings, or do I fret because I do not have someone else's? Am I careful to remain aware of my Father's constant goodness? Dear Lord, let me not fail to give thanks in everything. May I set an example for my children of eyes which see Your goodness to us and a heart which is grateful.*

*LOVE IS Jelly on the Bread*

# 19
# Fringe Benefits

Ever since we have required "dough" to make our children "college-bred" (forgive the pun—it's not my best!), my husband has worked a second job as an evening shift security guard. It is the kind of work in which the fringe benefits are as attractive as the pay—at least for a teacher and writer—because there are long, quiet periods during which he can study.

The most literal fringe benefit, however, surrounds the fringes of the property where he is working. For several weeks in mid-summer, wild blackberry bushes hang heavy with large, plump fruit. Every evening while the daylight lasts, he picks berries as he walks the perimeter (which is acceptable to the owners, of course, and no one else seems interested in the fruit). Night after night he brings home anywhere from a pint to two quarts. Needless to say, while the season lasts they become a mainstay of our menus. We have blackberries on breakfast cereal and in mixed fruit bowls. They appear as dessert over ice cream, or with milk and sugar, or as an upside-down cake.

During this season I make several batches of jam.

It is more than we can possibly eat, but I always have a special feeling of gratitude to the Lord when I have something I can give away. The occasions for doing so are many—a hostess gift, a Christmas greeting, a food shower for a missionary coming home on furlough.

These berries are not our only source of jams and jellies. Our own backyard has furnished us with beautiful surprises for which the deed of sale did not prepare us. There is an apple tree that provides an abundance of jelly, applesauce, pies, brown Bettys and other desserts every fall.

From some patches of mint I make at least one batch of jelly every spring. It is far tastier served with lamb than is the apple-mint you buy in the stores and it is always an appreciated gift to lamb lovers. I had never thought of it as a breakfast jelly, but my son-in-law likes it spread on his toast. And, of course, the sprigs of mint add dash to iced tea and lemonade all summer.

There is also a cherry tree and a grapevine of which we were not even aware until we had lived here two or three years. It is a fringe benefit discovered by my brother-in-law some years ago. The insignificant-looking little stem which he found growing at the back of the yard did not look to me like something worth getting excited about, but he erected posts and string and aimed the stem in their direction.

That fall it produced a few deliciously sweet, deep purple grapes. Now, more than a dozen years later, that unassuming little stem forms a fence on two sides of our garden and provides us with a winter's supply of marvelous grape juice, plus all the jelly I have the inclination and sugar to make.

One of our most surprising bonuses has to be the plum tree. For about three years after we moved in, it just stood there barren and ugly in an out-of-the-way corner. One day one of the children rammed it with a lawn mower so that it cracked and fell, revealing itself to be only a hollow dead thing. My husband finished cutting it down and we forgot about it.

Many summers later we noticed a few shoots sprouting from the old stump. The following year it presented us with a handful of small but sweet prune plums. The next year there was a large bowl of plums. Last summer we harvested more than we could eat, enough that I experimented with both freezing and canning them. I am still a little awed at the miracle of the plum tree.

Sometimes our fringe benefits come as gifts. I have a lovely sister-in-law down South who sends us a large bag of shelled pecans at Christmas. I love doing my holiday cooking with them, especially starting out with a batch of my husband's favorite pecan sticky buns. They are one of my favorite Christmas presents, usually lasting into the spring.

At other times the little lady who owns the roadside stand where George regularly picks up eggs has bestowed the fringe benefit. She keeps one counter of produce that has to move fast and is therefore marked at a dollar, or often fifty cents, a basket. Perhaps she had noticed us regularly and carefully shopping that counter. At any rate, she asked us one day if we would care to take home and look over a basket she was about to discard.

I thought, "What can we lose?" and accepted it. When I went through it, I found a couple of very ripe melons (always the sweetest to my way of thinking), some cucumbers soft at the tip but otherwise firm and fresh tasting, and a quantity of nectarines which were brown and soft on one side, but firm on the other. They made a large, tasty bowlful.

Since then, my husband has often brought in a bag of assorted fruits or vegetables along with the eggs. Somehow, these extra bounties seem to coincide with the week college tuition is due or the budget is otherwise pinching particularly hard. More than once I have said a prayer of thanksgiving for that little woman.

There have been occasions, too, when fringe benefits have come even more directly as an act of God. A peach tree stood on the property where George worked. It was unusually heavy with fruit one fall and, just as they were ripe, a bolt of lightning uprooted the tree. He brought home basket after basket of peaches, even though other employees were also picking. We ate fresh peaches for days, and those I canned and froze lasted the entire winter.

I remember how my grandmother used to say, "The Lord gave me one of His exceedingly abundantlies today." When she was still around, the term "fringe benefit" had not come into common usage. I think she may have had the better expression. These unplanned bounties, that are certainly an expression of His love beyond our basic provisions, have a way of making life, as well as meal-planning, a series of small adventures. They are wonderful, too, for keeping alive whatever small spark of creativity we may have as we find ways to use and vary them.

It is also possible to create a few fringe benefits for ourselves by being alert for small methods of saving that can add up to big bonuses. One of our few extravagances is bacon. Though I may stay away from it for weeks at a time, I find it impossible to pass up a good sale without buying a pound. This is especially true when our tomatoes are abundant, for we love bacon-tomato sandwiches. When I buy a package, I cut off half an inch or so from each end. Nobody misses the ends, but I have them available for one of the many dishes—wilted lettuce, for example, or German potato salad—to which diced bacon makes the perfect addition.

I save every drop of bacon fat. It adds its flavor to onions, eggs, hamburger patties, French toast, and a dozen or more other things that can be fried in it. The fat can be cut into biscuits and used for the melted fat called for in some waffle and pancake recipes. Ham fat and rendered chicken fat are equally delicious and versatile. Of course, these would not be practical for people under medical orders to avoid animal fats, but for us it is a small saving and a big flavor bonus.

I always save the wrappers on margarine, for there is nothing better to grease pans with. I keep them handy in a plastic container and they don't even have to be refrigerated if one bakes frequently.

Whenever possible, before I use an orange or a lemon, I grate the rind. These grated peels have countless delicious uses, especially in baking. One of my favorite touches is to mix a grated rind with sugar for sprinkling on the top of glazed cookies. If your gratings will not be used within a few days, they should be stored in the freezer because they mold quickly. Because of their acidity, they should also be stored in glass rather than plastic containers.

The crumbs that can be scraped from cake and

cookie pans after baking, or that accumulate on the cake plate or in the bottom of the cookie jar are too useful to throw away. They gradually dry out and keep indefinitely in a covered container. I use them as I would a bread crumb topping on a dessert. If you do not have enough cookie crumbs by themselves, bread crumbs can be mixed with them. They can also be mixed with or substituted for graham cracker or cornflake crumbs.

I almost never throw away the rind of a watermelon. It makes marvelous gourmet pickles that will give you somewhat of a claim to fame because so few people do it. I make at least one batch every summer. Probably most any complete cookbook would have a recipe for it. The one I use is quite basic. I peel and remove all green and red portions of the watermelon rinds and cut them into about one-inch cubes. The cubes should be soaked overnight in a salt water solution of one fourth cup of salt and four cups of water in a covered container. Drain thoroughly the next day and cover with clean cold water. Simmer until rinds are almost tender. Drain thoroughly.

In a large kettle combine eight cups sugar, four cups vinegar, and spices (which should be tied in a cheesecloth), two tablespoons cloves, five sticks cinnamon, two tablespoons allspice. Bring to a boil and simmer uncovered five minutes. Let the mixture cool about fifteen minutes, then add drained watermelon rind cubes and simmer until they are translucent. Discard spice bag and pack cubes and liquid immediately in clean, hot jars and seal.

Sometimes, if I make several batches of the watermelon rind pickles, I will tint one green and another red. These are especially nice to have at Christmastime, both for your own table and to give as gifts.

A useful trick I owe to my husband is one my children have labeled (a little derisively) "The Syme Mix." We keep the juices left from pickles. Whenever we empty a mayonnaise or mustard jar, or any bottled dressing, we pour in a little pickle juice and shake vigorously, gleaning all the flavor from the sides. It can then be flavored further as desired—George loves to experiment with various seasonings—and used in tossed salad. If a thicker dressing is desired a tablespoon or so of mayonnaise can be added. Ketchup and meat sauce bottles can be finished off the same way, but I have usually rinsed them into tomato or barbecue sauce before he gets hold of them.

It would be difficult indeed to remember all the fringe benefits the Lord has sent our way through the years. These are only samples. Yours may be very different and may come to you in different forms. I am sure that we are not alone in being such recipients of love gifts from Heaven to brighten our table. But, perhaps, through the years the Lord has taught us to cultivate an awareness of them and a thankfulness of heart to receive them. If so, that is undoubtedly the greatest benefit of all.

# 20
# Bounty to Share

Jesus said, "It is more blessed to give than to receive" (Acts 20:35). There are times when it can also be as much fun. I am always grateful and accepting when someone wants to share his bounty with us. I enjoy it even more when I have bounty to share with someone else.

With a little planning, it becomes possible to depend on one's shelves and freezer to be the unfailing source of attractive and acceptable greetings—a food offering to a hostess, a bit of cheer to a shut-in, a food shower, and of course, Christmas gifts are always available and appreciated. I usually have opportunities to make assorted jams and jellies. With this in mind, I am an inveterate jar saver. Instant coffee, mustard, honey and similar groceries come in really handsome jars. When I have two or three exactly alike, I make a point of putting a different kind of jam or jelly in each. Then, if I am giving more than one jar, I have a nice set.

Most pickles and relishes require sealing in Mason jars so I occasionally have to purchase a carton of these as my supply dwindles. My favorite for gifting, unless to a large family, is the half-pint size which in recent years has been manufactured in attractive shapes and designs.

Baked goods are another fun item to give as well as receive. One of our most interesting gifts last Christmas came from a woman who baked about five thousand cookies as gifts. The ones we received were packed in a half-gallon ice cream tub—one of the plastic ones with a transparent lid. At the very top, carefully arranged to be read through the lid, were three special cookies. A package-shaped one was inscribed with the words, "Merry Christmas" and two others, a boy and a girl, were decorated with "George" and "Charlotte."

The remainder of the box was a perpetual surprise package. There were scarcely more than three or four cookies exactly alike. In size, shape, color, flavor, it was a treasure chest of new discoveries all the way to the bottom. It was a real delight for the receiver, and I am sure a fun gift for the giver as well.

I occasionally make cookies for giving, but I prefer making breads and cakes. I save coffee cans, large tin orange juice cans, and any other suitably-shaped tin cans or aluminum foil pans that come into my hands. When our budget can handle it, I like to make fruit cakes in the fall. My favorite one has an apple-sauce base which makes it deliciously moist and, since I make several dozen jars of applesauce from our own tree every year, it is more economical than most. I have used this recipe for so long that I do not know where I first got it.

Mix together three cups of hot applesauce, one cup butter and two cups of sugar; let stand overnight. Combine four teaspoons soda, four and one half cups flour, one teaspoon each of nutmeg, cloves and salt. Sift this mixture to coat the following: one box raisins, one pound snipped dates, one large box diced, candied, mixed fruit, one half pound pecans or walnuts. Sift the rest of the flour mixture into the applesauce, add the fruit and nut mixture, and mix all together thoroughly. Divide into several greased and floured containers. I use various sizes of loaf pans, ring molds, the cans and other containers mentioned above, and even small muffin cups for individual fruitcakes. Bake in a slow oven about 50 minutes; less for very small containers.

Before baking, the tops of the cakes can be attractively decorated with candied cherries or other fruits and nuts. Or they can be iced after baking. A butter cream frosting, white or tinted, or if desired, decorated with colorful pieces of candied cherry or other fruit or nuts, looks nice. These cakes keep in the refrigerator for months and in the freezer indefinitely. They are nice for holiday entertaining and for giving.

Some other favorites for quantity baking are cranberry-orange and a pumpkin bread. Purchase cranberries on sale and freeze until needed. Practically every cookbook has recipes for these, but the cranberry recipe I have found most delicious is the one printed on the bag they are packaged in. Pumpkin recipes abound in both yeast and quick bread versions. Both these items are less expensive to make than fruitcake.

For even more economy, try an applesauce-orange-nut bread. I use any standard applesauce-nut bread recipe and add a tablespoon of grated orange rind and a teaspoon of orange extract. This bread is almost as good when raisins are substituted for the nuts.

All these cakes and breads may be removed from their pans, wrapped in foil and frozen. The foil itself looks very Christmasy when a red or green ribbon is tied around it.

Avoid the crowds and do your Christmas shopping leisurely from your own pantry shelves! As a bonus, you are in practically no danger of choosing something unusable or wrong in color or size. You will probably even avoid duplicating someone else's gift. But if not, it won't matter. The more the tastier!

*To meditate on: Am I careful to be aware of the opportunities for sharing my life and bounty with others? Lord, help me to remember the blessings of both giving and receiving.*

*LOVE IS Jelly on the Bread*

# 21
# Big Dividends with
# Small Extras

Preparing suitable meals day after day within a rather rigid budget can be pure drudgery, or it can be a challenge. Ways of meeting the challenge will vary according to one's income and the personal tastes of the family. The suggestions presented here have worked for me. They may be applicable to your household, or they may merely be catalysts to stir your imagination.

Flavor, variety and eye appeal can be added to even the least expensive dishes. For this purpose, I try to keep on hand a few pet extravagances which are not really extravagant at all when one considers how long they will last. Of course, I purchase them only if the basics have been cared for.

Olives would probably head my "extravagance" list. A jar of the broken salad olives costs about a dollar and a half and lasts many weeks. Not only are cream cheese and olive sandwiches among our lunch-box favorites, but the pimento in the jar can be used for other purposes. Canned black olives are almost as practical, making an interesting addition to a number of casseroles and salads. The medium size is a better buy than the large and works just as well, either halved or sliced.

If I possibly can, I take advantage of every sale on canned stems and pieces of mushrooms. I try to save them for special occasions or company meals. They are the most delicious way I know to glamorize and stretch inexpensive hamburger, beef, and some chicken dishes.

Sour cream is another favorite. I prefer the imitation version of this to the genuine article. It is less expensive, contains less butterfat and fewer calories, and keeps several times longer in the refrigerator. It will do anything real sour cream will do. In our area, the standard price is fifty-nine cents a pint, but it frequently goes on sale. Sour cream is a must for making stroganoff, but that is not its only use, of course. It is an excellent dressing for vegetables and can be varied in flavor with any number of gourmet touches. Try it mixed with mustard or cheese over boiled cabbage, broccoli, beans or other vegetables. Or mix with poppy seeds, dill or parsley to top carrots, cabbage or boiled new potatoes. It is a good base for salad dressings and dips. Your cookbook will yield many suggestions.

Nuts are probably the most expensive of all my pet extras, but even with these, a little can go a long way. I enjoy my Christmas-gift pecans best in breads, cookies and cakes. Mixed with brown sugar and margarine, they make a marvelous topping for fruit or pumpkin pies and also for baked, mashed squash.

I try to keep a package of slivered almonds on hand. Browned in a little margarine, they can turn a dish of vegetables into something special. Try them over green beans, or broccoli that has been tossed with plain sour cream. They are also very nice in chop suey, especially if the bits of meat are minimal. A generous sprinkling of broken cashews in a tuna or poultry salad or casserole can turn it into company fare.

A less costly substitute for nuts is water chestnuts. They are not just for chop suey. Try slicing a couple into a pan of green or wax beans, or cooked greens. They add a nice crunch as well as a brightened appearance. Like almonds, they can be sauteed lightly in margarine before adding to anything. A small can costs about fifty-nine cents, but contains enough for three or four uses and can be kept in the freezer after opening.

Not all extras have to come from the grocery shelves. Your own windowsill can supply some real goodies. As I write this on a very wintery March day during a heavy snowfall, my husband is boasting of being a papa to five tomatoes.

The story is this. We had a tomato plant especially bred for city balconies left over from some he had potted as a birthday gift for our daughter. He put it in a large old pail to be a replacement if one of hers died. All summer it sat on the porch and produced two nice handfuls of small tomatoes. In the fall he set it in a sunny window to see what would happen.

Now, tomatoes will not set fruit unless the blossoms are cross pollinated, a necessity normally taken care of by bees. Indoors that presented a problem. When a few blossoms appeared, George tickled their centers with a small artist's brush. Some time later, we began to notice five tiny green balls of fruit which are now growing steadily and sturdily. Long before it is time to set any plants outdoors, we should be dressing up a salad or two with fresh tomatoes.

My sunniest windowsills also contain a pot of celery tops and a window box of parsley. The celery plant was a gift and an exciting new discovery to me. I keep breaking branches off and new ones promptly grow up to replace them. They are a real treat chopped into salads or added to the makings of soup stock. I grow parsley all year round—outdoors in summer and inside in winter.

Sometimes we also have chives, lettuce and radishes in boxes. One does not get a great deal of lettuce this way, but a little tossed with purchased iceberg and other greens adds a lot to a salad. And there is nothing like the cheery redness of a few slices of radish peeking through your salad greens to remind you that winter is not going to last forever. The chives are a good flavor substitute for onions.

Another little extra that makes a meal look lavish and brings pleasant exclamations from guests is a smorgasbord of relishes. The exact makeup will vary from time to time. At this moment, I have on my shelves six varieties of pickles that I made entirely from my own or friends' excess produce. They include beet, green tomato, two varieties of cucumber, watermelon, and a hot dog relish made mostly of green tomatoes and peppers. Not long ago I also had pickled crabapples and chowchow which were Christmas gifts.

In addition to the pickles I have red and yellow tomato jams and green tomato marmalade. These are all delicious served with dinner as you would cranberry sauce. The marmalade is also good for breakfast on English muffins.

Any two or three of these items chosen for variety of color, texture and flavor is sure to lend interest and pleasure to your meal. At a holiday or family dinner, I usually set out a tray of everything I have because of the wide variety of tastes that exist among my children and their spouses.

Sometimes your extra dividends will require the expenditure of a little time instead of money. Some jams and fruits served in a cut glass dish have the look of a jewel. An assortment or balance of color in the arrangement of nibblers makes one want to reach for them. Study the way they are served at a catered or restaurant banquet and adapt the ideas to your own food and tableware. It takes only a few minutes to cut radishes into fans or rosettes, or shave carrots into curls, but it adds much to their eye appeal.

Plan centerpieces; they add so much to a table. My husband shines in this department. He has always kept me provided with two centerpieces—one for the dining room and one for the kitchen table. He uses whatever flowers are blooming. If there are few, he can always find enough green stuff to fill them out. Mint is beautiful and fragrant in a table bouquet. But be warned, it grows in the dish!

Over the years he has collected containers suitable to different seasons and different kinds of flowers. From those special occasions when he has brought home florists' arrangements, he has kept the non-perishable additions they often include and used them to decorate his own efforts. He has gradually built up a collection of attractive artificial flowers for those times when nothing is growing. In some seasons, arrangements of fruit are possible. Late summer vegetables with their varied shapes and beautiful colors are also perfectly beautiful.

Little things add so much.

# 22
# The Greatest Meal

Hanging on our dining room wall is a picture given to us several years ago by the students in our Bible classes. The scene is that of a banquet table, richly set and stretching back into infinity. Etched below it are the words, "Come, for all things are now ready." It is one of my favorite possessions.

The Scripture tells us that there is coming an occasion when the Lord Jesus will host a great feast at which the invited guests will be all those who have acknowledged Him on this earth. The Apostle John called it, "the marriage supper of the Lamb."

We can only be eligible for this Heavenly feast, however, if we have received the wonderful gift of life He proffers us. This is the truest gift of love the world has ever known. It is no light "fun gift," but one costly and painful beyond all comprehension.

It took His bruised and broken body to produce the bread for a life that is both eternal and abundant. It is eternal because no one can take it from us, and abundant because it does not depend on the material advantages of this world to make it joyful and fulfilling. Those who have this life recognize that the truly rich are those who are privileged to love and be loved, to know and express gratitude, and to render service.

If you do not have this life, you are missing the best. You can receive it as you would any gift. Accept it from the nail-scarred hand of the One who died the death your sins deserve in order to give you His eternal life. To "as many as received him [Jesus Christ], to them gave he power to become the sons of God, even to them that believe on his name" (John 1:12). "He that heareth my word, and believeth on him that sent me, hath everlasting life, and shall not come into condemnation; but is passed from death unto life" (John 5:24).

To care for the physical sustenance of those whom the Lord has entrusted to us, no matter how beautifully and lovingly we do it, is only part of our responsibility. We hope we have set forth in these pages something of the importance of preparing and serving the bread of life along with the bread of this earth.

*To meditate on: Hopefully, these pages will enrich and brighten the daily tasks of some. But if they encourage someone to set her feet on the path of life and walk with the Giver of Life, nourishing those in her care for both time and eternity, the author's joy will overflow. Lord, may it be so.*